NFL TEAM STORIES

The Story of the

NEW YORK GIANTS

By Jim Gigliotti

Kaleidoscope
Minneapolis, MN

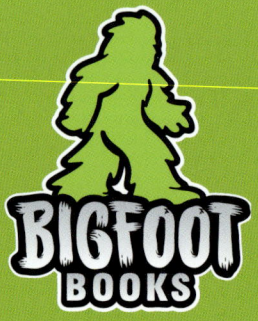

The Quest for Discovery Never Ends

···

This edition first published in 2021 by Kaleidoscope Publishing, Inc.

No part of this publication may be reproduced in whole or in part without written permission of the publisher.

For information regarding permission, write to
Kaleidoscope Publishing, Inc.
6012 Blue Circle Drive
Minnetonka, MN 55343

Library of Congress Control Number
2020935948

ISBN
978-1-64519-240-4 (library bound)
978-1-64519-308-1 (ebook)

Text copyright © 2021 by Kaleidoscope Publishing, Inc. All-Star Sports, Bigfoot Books, and associated logos are trademarks and/or registered trademarks of Kaleidoscope Publishing, Inc.

Printed in the United States of America.

FIND ME IF YOU CAN!

Bigfoot lurks within one of the images in this book. It's up to you to find him!

TABLE OF CONTENTS

Kickoff! 4

Chapter 1: Giants History 6

Chapter 2: Giants All-Time Greats 16

Chapter 3: Giants Superstars 22

Beyond the Book 28
Research Ninja 29
Further Resources 30
Glossary 31
Index 32
Photo Credits 32
About the Author 32

KICKOFF!

The Giants have been around almost as long as the NFL—but not quite! The NFL began in 1920. At first, the league had no team in New York. That is hard to

FUN FACT
NFL kickoffs are now taken at the 35-yard line.

believe! New York is America's biggest city. It was the biggest city in 1920, too! The Giants finally came along in 1925. There might not be an NFL today without them. The team helped save the league. How did they do it? Read on!

The NFL's Giants took their name from an MLB team called the New York Giants. That team moved to San Francisco in 1958.

Chapter 1
Giants History

The NFL had a tough time in its early days. Some teams did not make it and had to stop playing. The Giants started playing in 1925. They had trouble finding fans, however.

On December 6, the Giants played an **exhibition game** against the Chicago Bears. A huge crowd of 73,000 people showed up to watch at Yankee Stadium. It was the first time pro football was a big deal. Everyone wanted to be there. Thanks to the game, the Giants survived. A successful team in New York meant the NFL survived. That is how the Giants helped save the NFL.

The Giants played lots of games in baseball ballparks. From 1925 to 1956, they played at the Polo Grounds, right.

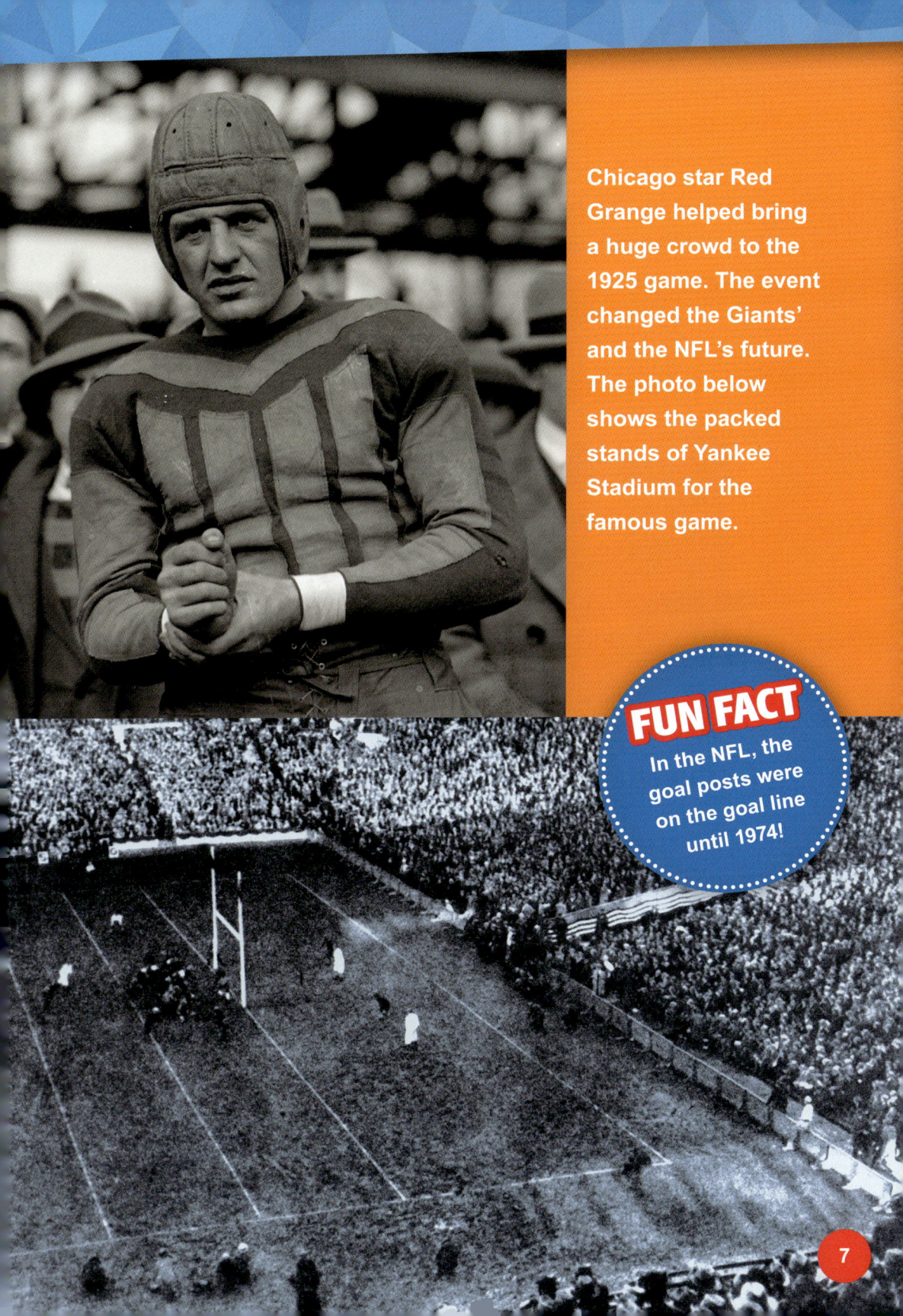

Chicago star Red Grange helped bring a huge crowd to the 1925 game. The event changed the Giants' and the NFL's future. The photo below shows the packed stands of Yankee Stadium for the famous game.

FUN FACT

In the NFL, the goal posts were on the goal line until 1974!

The Giants became really good really fast. They won the league title in 1927. That was only their third year in the NFL. They have been champions seven more times since.

THE SNEAKERS GAME

The Giants beat the Bears 30–13 for the 1934 NFL title. It is called the Sneakers Game. It is one of the most famous games ever. The Giants trailed at halftime. They put on basketball sneakers for the second half. The shoes helped them run better on the icy field. New York roared back to win!

Facemask-free action from the 1934 title game.

At first, the NFL champ was the team with the best record. In 1933, the NFL played its first Championship Game. The Giants lost that game to the Bears. They beat the Bears in the next year's game.

Phil Simms

The Giants were one of the best teams for a long time. They made the playoffs 16 times from 1933 to 1963. They were champs three times in that stretch. They made the title game three years in a row starting in 1961. That was the good news for Giants fans. They lost all three of those games. That was the bad news for Giants fans.

The team had a dry spell after that. No playoffs until 1981! Then in 1986, Bill Parcells coached the Giants to their first Super Bowl win. They won again in 1990. Parcells left after that. Tom Coughlin arrived in 2004. He coached the Giants for 12 seasons. He took the team to two more Super Bowls. Both games were against the New England Patriots. The Patriots were big **favorites** in both. The Giants won both!

Eli Manning

The Giants have not been very good since their last Super Bowl win in 2011. They made the playoffs only once. That was in 2016.

The Giants won only three games in 2017. The next two years were not much better. The team hired Joe Judge as coach in 2020. He was an assistant coach for the Patriots. He helped that team win three Super Bowls. The Giants hope he does the same in New York!

Daniel Jones

TIMELINE OF THE NEW YORK GIANTS

1925

1925: The Giants begin play.

1927

1927: The team wins its first NFL title.

1934

1934: The Giants win the famous "Sneakers Game."

1963

1963: The Giants play in their third title game in a row.

1986

1986: The team wins the Super Bowl for the first time.

2007

2007: The Giants stun the undefeated Patriots in the Super Bowl.

2020

2020: The team hires Joe Judge as its new head coach.

WHAT A CATCH!

14

The Giants shocked the Patriots in the Super Bowl in 2007. It was the Patriots' only loss all year. The Giants did it with an amazing catch.

The Giants trailed late in the game. It was third down. Quarterback Eli Manning faced a big rush. The Patriots grabbed him. Then Manning escaped! He threw the ball down the field. David Tyree leaped high. He was hit as he reached for the ball (far left). Tyree pressed the ball to the top of his helmet. He crashed hard to the ground. He held on to the ball for a 32-yard gain. Four plays later, the Giants scored a touchdown. They won 17–14. It was one of the most famous catches in NFL history. The win was also one of the biggest upsets!

Chapter 2
Giants All-Time Greats

Two of the best defensive stars ever played for the Giants. Lawrence Taylor was a linebacker. He joined the team in 1981. No one ever saw a player like him before. He could rush the passer. He could tackle the ball carrier. He could cover pass catchers. He did all of that better than anyone else before him—and maybe since!

Defensive end Michael Strahan was great at making **sacks**. He led the NFL in that stat twice. He had 22.5 sacks in 2001. That is the most ever in one season.

FUN FACT
Taylor's 20.5 sacks in 1986 were a team record until Strahan topped it in 2001.

Lawrence Taylor

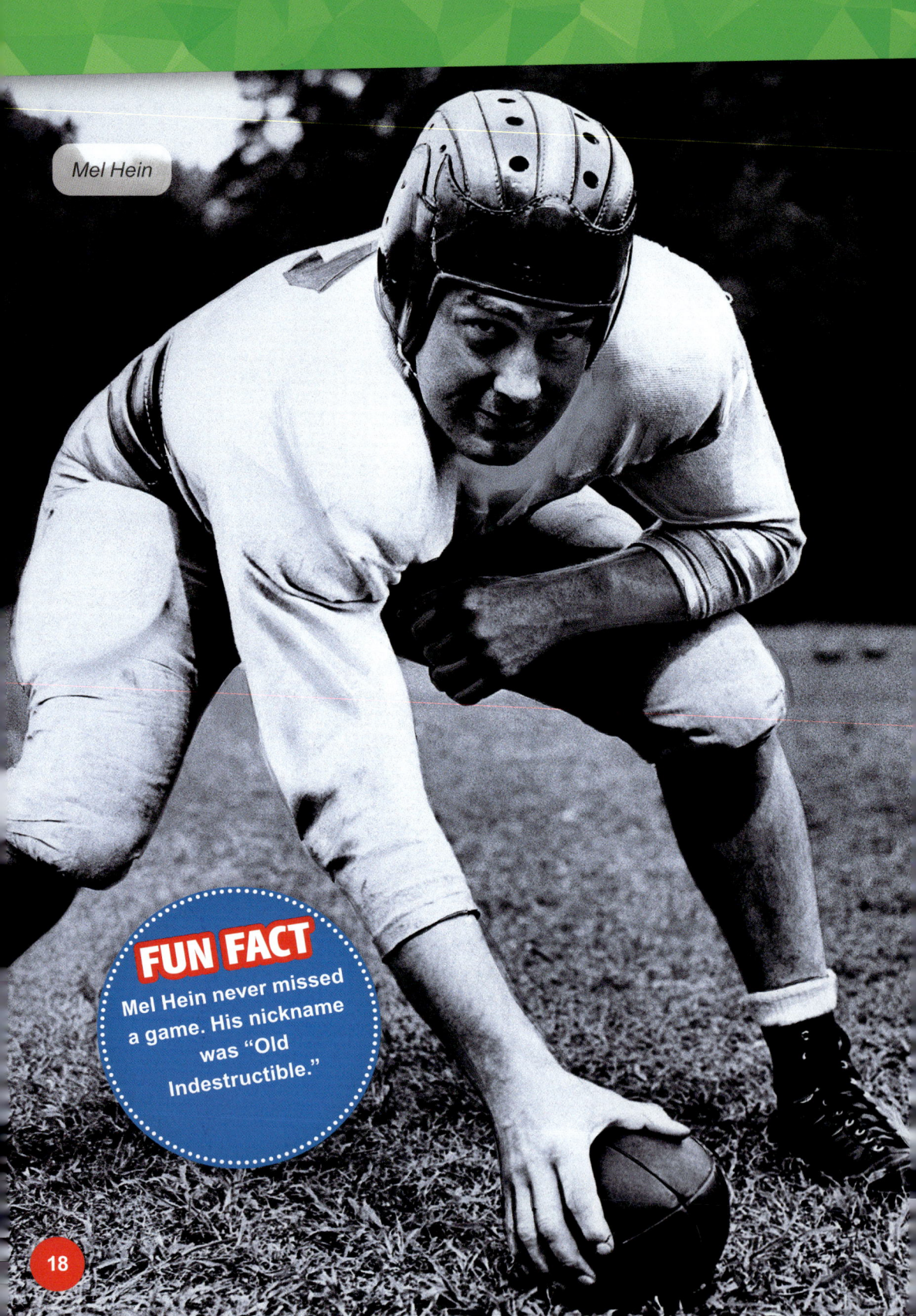

Mel Hein

FUN FACT
Mel Hein never missed a game. His nickname was "Old Indestructible."

The Giants have more than 30 Hall of Famers. Center Mel Hein was one of the greats in the early days. He never missed a game in high school, college, or the NFL!

Emlen Tunnell was one of the top safeties ever. He **intercepted** 74 passes for the team in the 1940s and 1950s. Frank Gifford was a great runner and pass catcher. He played in the 1950s and 1960s. Running back Tiki Barber joined the team in 1997. He gained more than 10,000 yards in 10 seasons.

Tiki Barber

The Giants have had many star quarterbacks, too. Benny Friedman was one of the NFL's first great passers. Charlie Conerly and Y.A. Tittle were **Pro Bowl** players. Phil Simms led the team to its first Super Bowl win.

Eli Manning passed for the most yards in team history. He passed for the most touchdowns, too. Manning led the Giants to two Super Bowl wins. He was the game's MVP both times.

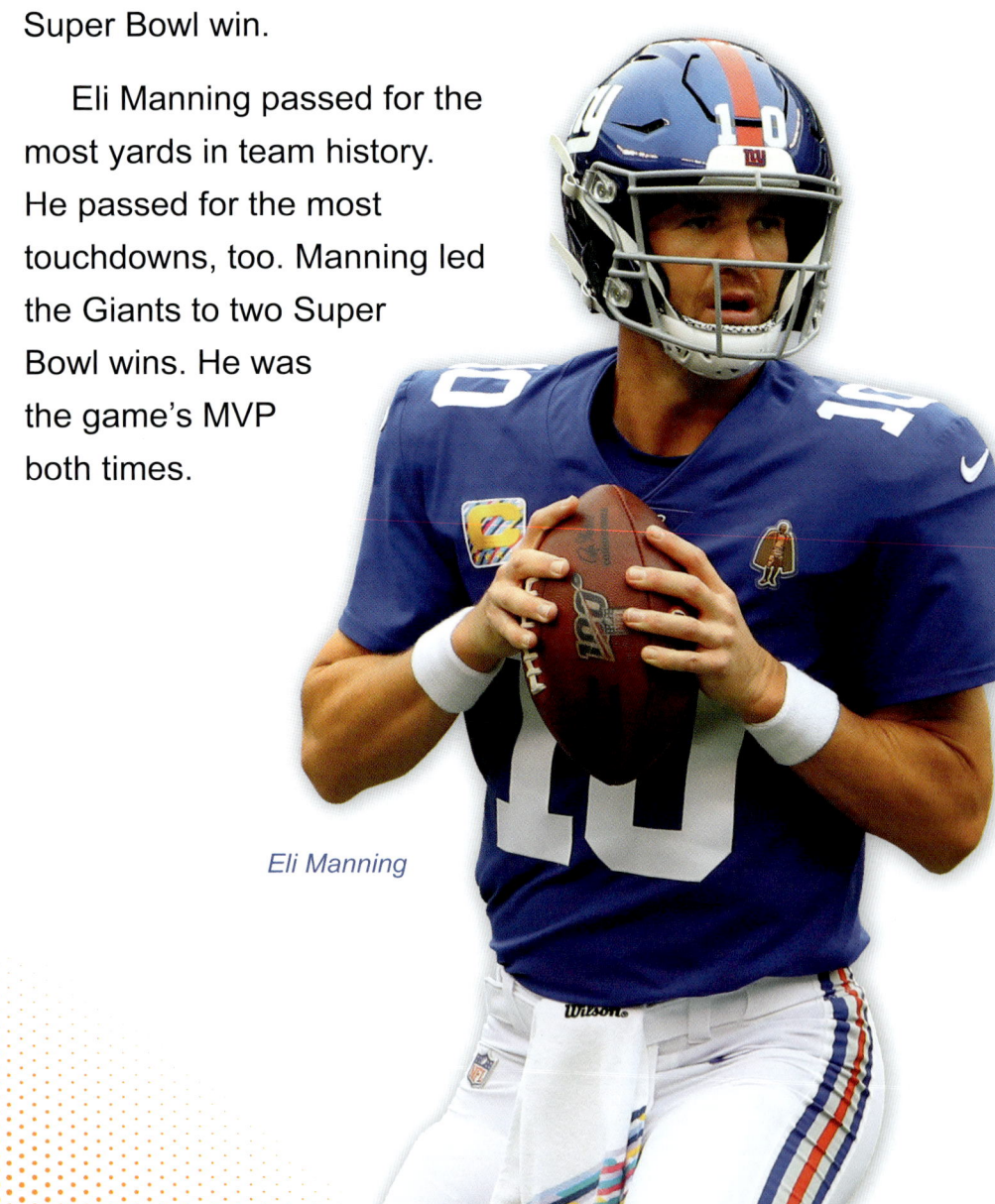

Eli Manning

GIANTS RECORDS

These players piled up the best stats in Giants history. The numbers are career records through the 2019 season.

Total TDs: Frank Gifford, 78

TD Passes: Eli Manning, 366

Passing Yards: Eli Manning, 57,023

Rushing Yards: Tiki Barber, 10,449

Receptions: Amani Toomer, 668

Points: Pete Gogolak, 646

Sacks: Michael Strahan, 141.5

Chapter 3
Giants Superstars

All-time great Eli Manning retired after the 2019 season. The Giants may have found their next big quarterback already. He is Daniel Jones. He was a huge star at Duke University. The Giants **drafted** Jones in the first round in 2019. He started 12 games as a **rookie**. He passed for 24 touchdowns. The team is excited to see what he can do in the future.

Daniel Jones

Evan Engram

Daniel Jones will get a lot of help from Saquon Barkley. He is a superstar running back. Barkley was drafted second overall in 2018. He led the NFL in yards from scrimmage as a rookie. That is rushing yards plus receiving yards. Barkley ran for more than 1,000 yards in '19.

Jones has many options when he passes. Sterling Shepard is a sure-handed receiver. Darius Slayton was better than anyone expected as a rookie in 2019. Evan Engram is a big tight end.

Jabrill Peppers

The Giants have good, young players on offense. They have to improve on defense. They will build around safety Jabrill Peppers. They got him in a key trade in 2019. Peppers is as big as a linebacker. He is as fast as a defensive back.

DeAndre Baker is a cornerback the Giants are counting on. They drafted him in the first round in 2019. He took some lumps early in his rookie season. Then he came on strong. Giants fans hope their team comes on strong in 2020, too!

DeAndre Baker

BEYOND THE BOOK

After reading the book, it's time to think about what you learned. Try the following exercises to jumpstart your ideas.

RESEARCH

FIND OUT MORE. Where would you go to find out more about your favorite NFL teams and players? Check out NFL.com, of course. Each team also has its own website. What other sports information sites can you find? See if you can find other cool facts about your favorite team.

CREATE

GET ARTISTIC. Each NFL team has a logo. The Giants logo shows the letters NY for New York. Get some art materials and try designing your own Giants logo. Or create a new team and make a logo for it. What colors would you choose? How would you draw the mascot?

DISCOVER

GO DEEP! This book features a story about an incredible, game-saving catch. Do some research and find some other amazing catches from NFL history. Did any of them win big games? Did any get their own special nicknames? What did they all have in common?

GROW

GET OUT AND PLAY! You don't need to be in the NFL to enjoy football. You just need a football and some friends. Play touch or tag football. Or you can hang cloth flags from your belt; grab the belt and make the "tackle." See who has the best arm to be quarterback. Who is the best receiver? Who can run the fastest? Time to play football!

RESEARCH NINJA

Visit www.ninjaresearcher.com/2404 to learn how to take your research skills and book report writing to the next level!

RESEARCH

DIGITAL LITERACY TOOLS

SEARCH LIKE A PRO
Learn about how to use search engines to find useful websites.

FACT OR FAKE?
Discover how you can tell a trusted website from an untrustworthy resource.

TEXT DETECTIVE
Explore how to zero in on the information you need most.

SHOW YOUR WORK
Research responsibly—learn how to cite sources.

WRITE

GET TO THE POINT
Learn how to express your main ideas.

PLAN OF ATTACK
Learn prewriting exercises and create an outline.

DOWNLOADABLE REPORT FORMS

Further Resources

BOOKS

Editors of Sports Illustrated Kids. *1st and 10 (Revised and Updated): Top 10 Lists of Everything in Football.* New York: Sports Illustrated Kids, 2016.

Martirano, Ron. *Football: Great Records, Weird Happenings, Odd Facts, Amazing Moments & Other Cool Stuff.* Watertown, Mass.: Imagine Publishing, 2015.

Whiting, Jim. *The Story of the New York Giants (NFL Today).* Mankato, Minn.: Creative Paperbacks, 2019.

WEBSITES

FACTSURFER

Factsurfer.com gives you a safe, fun way to find more information.

1. Go to www.factsurfer.com.
2. Enter "New York Giants" into the search box and click 🔍
3. Select your book cover to see a list of related websites.

Glossary

drafted: chosen in the NFL's annual meeting to choose college players. In 2020, the Giants drafted tackle Andrew Thomas with their first pick.

exhibition game: a game in which the results don't count in the standings. NFL teams play three or four exhibition games each season.

favorite: the team that is expected to win. The Patriots were favorites in the Super Bowl. But the Giants won!

intercepted: when a defender catches a pass aimed at the offense. Tunnell stepped in front of the receiver and intercepted the ball.

Pro Bowl: the NFL's annual all-star game. The great Lawrence Taylor was honored with 10 Pro Bowl selections.

rookie: a player in his or her first season as a pro. Daniel Jones was the starting QB even though he was a rookie.

sacks: tackles of the quarterback behind the line of scrimmage. Michael Strahan was one of the NFL's best sack masters.

upset: a game won by a team that was expected to lose. The Giants beat the Patriots in the Super Bowl in a huge upset.

Index

Baker, DeAndre, 27
Barber, Tiki, 19
Barkley, Saquon, 25
Chicago Bears, 6, 9
Conerly, Charlie, 20
Engram, Evan, 25
Friedman, Benny, 20
Gifford, Frank, 19
Hein, Mel, 19
Jones, Daniel, 22, 25
Judge, Joe, 12
Manning, Eli, 15, 20, 22

New England Patriots, 11, 12, 15
Parcells, Bill, 11
Peppers, Jabrill, 26
Shepard, Sterling, 25
Simms, Phil, 20
Slayton, Darius, 25
Strahan, Michael, 16
Super Bowl, 11, 12, 15, 20
Taylor, Lawrence, 16
Tittle, Y.A., 20
Tyree, David, 15

PHOTO CREDITS

The images in this book are reproduced through the courtesy of: AP Images: Pro Football Hall of Fame 6, 9; Reed Saxon 10; Mark Lennihan 16; 18. Focus on Football: 12, 19, 22, 24, 25. Library of Congress: 5. Newscom: Sam Riche/MCT 11; Karl Mondon/MCT 14; Pat Benic/UPI 15; Rich Graessle/Icon SW 6, 20, 26; Matthew Healey/UPI 27. Shutterstock: Debby Won 4. **Cover photo:** Focus on Football.

About the Author

Jim Gigliotti was an editor at NFL Publishing for many years. Now he writes books for young readers.